FROM

Embers

AND *Ash*

A Collection of Poems about
Heartache, Transformation
and Healing Trauma

Veronika Childs

First published in 2022
Written by Veronika Childs
Book design by Bryony van der Merwe

ISBN: 979-8-9869463-3-7 (paperback)
ISBN: 979-8-9869463-4-4 (ebook)

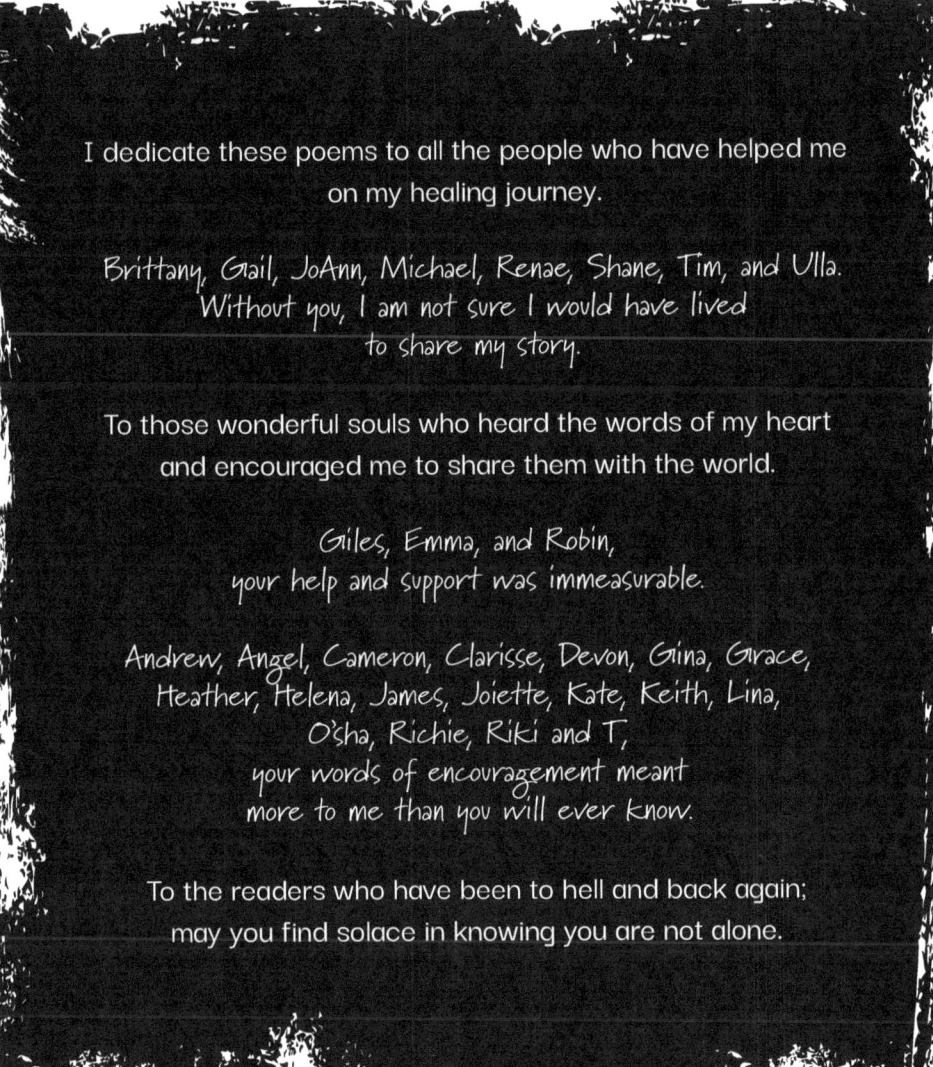

I dedicate these poems to all the people who have helped me
on my healing journey.

Brittany, Gail, JoAnn, Michael, Renae, Shane, Tim, and Ulla.
Without you, I am not sure I would have lived
to share my story.

To those wonderful souls who heard the words of my heart
and encouraged me to share them with the world.

Giles, Emma, and Robin,
your help and support was immeasurable.

Andrew, Angel, Cameron, Clarisse, Devon, Gina, Grace,
Heather, Helena, James, Joiette, Kate, Keith, Lina,
O'sha, Richie, Riki and T,
your words of encouragement meant
more to me than you will ever know.

To the readers who have been to hell and back again;
may you find solace in knowing you are not alone.

TRIGGER WARNING:

The poems contained in this book speak of life, loss, love,
and childhood trauma. I trust that you will follow your gut
when it comes to engaging with my words.

FROM *Embers* AND *Ash*

Who are we?
To you and me:
Mom, child
playful and wild
Woman, wife
In another life,
Whore
How can you adore
a mirage of what is,
a shadow of what was?
Who died
when she became his?

The truth
I should tell,
of evil and hell,
the girl, the child
so tender and mild,
became the whore
you would deplore

Identity

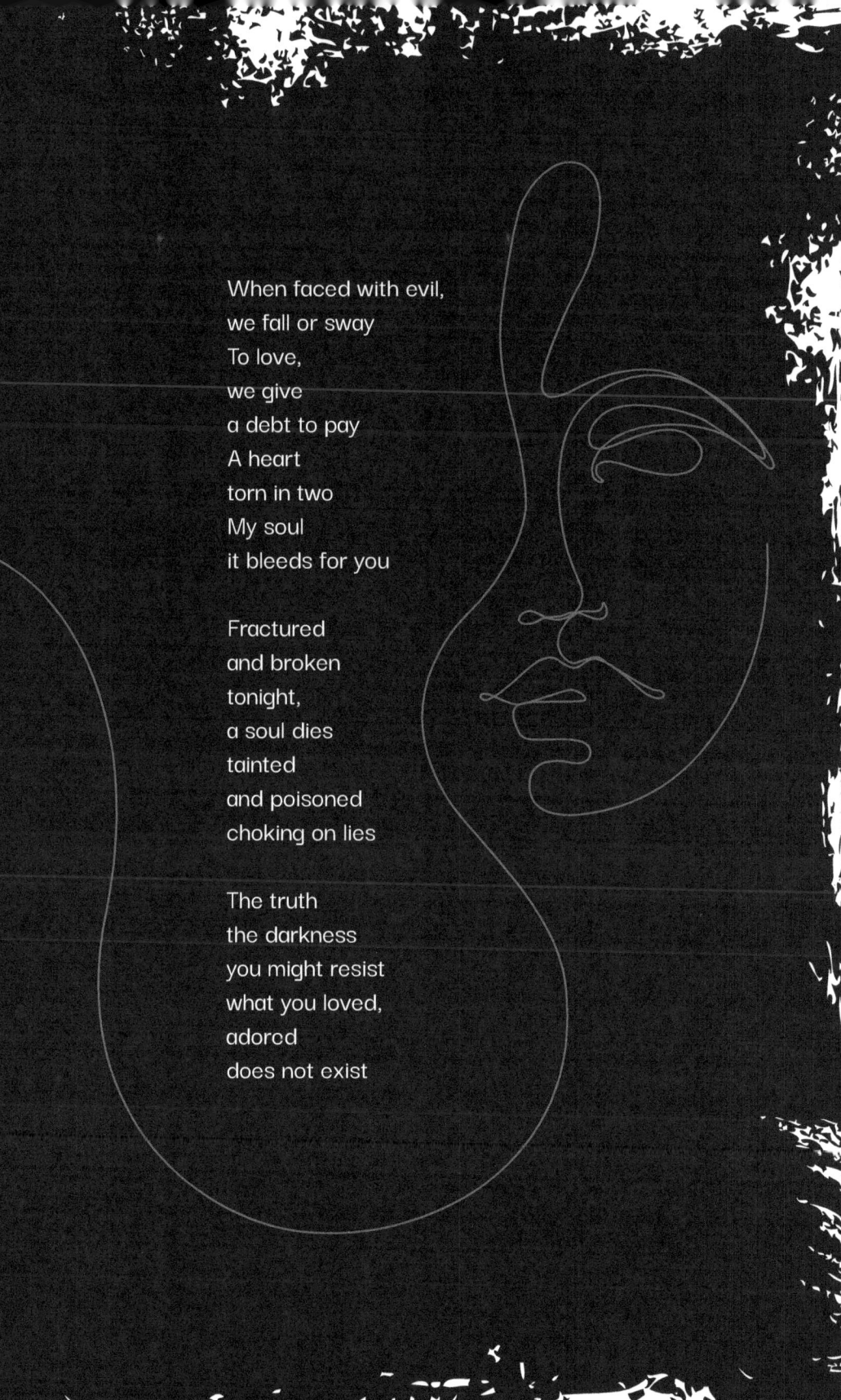

When faced with evil,
we fall or sway
To love,
we give
a debt to pay
A heart
torn in two
My soul
it bleeds for you

Fractured
and broken
tonight,
a soul dies
tainted
and poisoned
choking on lies

The truth
the darkness
you might resist
what you loved,
adored
does not exist

Perception distorted
Truth and lies sorted
and labeled, unstable
What's real?
What should I feel
when the illusions,
the false conclusions
crumble with the sands of time
and, the screams from a silent crime
still haunt my mind?

When you refuse to be blind,
will you be surprised to find
the truth is no more than a fantasy,
nowhere close to ecstasy
When truths and lies blend
and the thoughts they send
my heart and soul to its wit's end,
and my world spins
out of control,
I feel everything
and nothing at all.

When delusions fall,
isn't that the goal?
Inception
The past,
deception
The present
The future
The preconception
Everything takes a toll
On my perception

Perception

Perfection, perception
From the outside
looking in
Detection, deflection
of the shadows within
Smile, paint another mask
Denial, complete another task
Don't quit, give in
Don't you know how
lucky you are to live in
This world
so great, so sweet
Forget, regret
a moment of defeat
Guzzled and muzzled
then put on display
Remember to smile
Remember to play

Perfection

A Mile in my Shoes

Can you see the tears
behind the smile?
Would you take the time
to walk a mile
with my weighted shoes?
Or, those who you
unjustly choose
to judge, to label
to determine our fate?
A preconceived notion
it's all a mistake
With one glance
or a look
you take and don't give
compassion or grace
a chance to forgive
So much more
Nothing less than
today
and our history
Our hopes
and our dreams
to you
are a mystery

10

The road we walk
Where bridges burn
Where demons talk
and stomachs churn
It's more than just
an uphill battle
Don't you see?
We are branded and bought,
and traded like cattle

So, before you judge
and close the book
take a beat,
take a second look
Can you see the slaughter,
the struggle
behind the smile?
If you take the time
to walk a mile
in my shoes?

What is love?
patience and kindness
given to a child
encouragement to draw a smile
What would it be
to give a love so pure and free?

Yet, in my heart, I know
I scold and scorn every mistake,
keep track of failures and pills to take-
It's hard to swallow
to know
there's proof
I am not enough

What is love
given to others
but not to keep?
How can you give
what you still seek?

Love

What is love?
It starts and ends with you
Rejoice with the truth that you are you
and who you are is exactly
who you were meant to be
Perhaps there were other paths to see
but what is now just is

Love of self
   does not mean all is said and done
      change is never-ending
         love what is, and what will come.

         Trust. Hope. Persevere.

When Lights Fade

How sad to see
a light fade
before its time
Why do some
inherit the earth
and some get left behind
in the dust?
Left out in the cold,
until they rust
There seems to be no
rhyme or reason
to this time or season
Everyone has a struggle
yet some shoulder a burden
that would shatter most
A falling star,
before it fades,
burns bright
for all to see
Make a wish-
What will it be?
A hope for you and me

14

Your words,
like stones in water,
ripple through
my heart,
distorting truths,
altering beliefs
I am not enough
I am not worth saving
That is
just a lie
When I sit
in stillness,
and the ripples dissipate,
I can see
with clarity
Your words are
a reflection
of you—
not me

Your Words

15

In the dead of night,
when shadows rise
and nothing quiets,
the voices that whisper
forget me not
Who am I to decide
who should live
and who should die?
Is it time to say goodbye
to another life,
to another dream
of what could have been?

In the dead of night,
on a moonless stormy night,
when light is
but a memory,
who am I to say
what is real
and what is
just a dream?

In the Dead of Night

Is it time to wake up
in another life
to another fantasy
of what could have been?

In the dead of night,
when hope seems lost
when dreams disintegrate
who am I to say:
don't fret
there's a dawn
yet to be seen
It is time to say goodbye
Forget what could have been
Just be

In the dead of night

Hallowed
yet weighted
Panting
and sated
Chosen
Confused
Trapped
but removed

Don't fret, nothing is real

Disgusted
Delighted
Shamed
and excited
Enchanted
Recanted
Truths and lies
Slanted

Regret, nothing is real

Frozen
I'm fading
Sheer terror
Invading
Vanished
Evading
The monster
is waiting

Cold sweat, nothing is real

Anguish

Defiled
Defaced
Discarded
Erased
Disturbed
and distressed
Perturbed
and Repressed

My debt, nothing is real

Upset, nothing is real

No threat, nothing is real

Nothing is real

I am
        nothing

Grief never sleeps
and dreams never last
Yet I cannot weep
for a time, long past

When fragments of you
and my demons fight
When memories
of monsters
still
haunt the night

There's a truth
locked in my head
What you did,
what you said...
How it felt
to flee
When snarls lurk
and smiles melt,
I ceased to be
the love you used
and refused to see

I trusted you, loved you
and you threw me away
Dismayed, broken-hearted
Destroyed and discarded
Unused, I was useless
To you, I was worthless

Could you foresee
your actions would remain
A permanent stain
imprinted on me
Or were you blind
to see the damage done,
when you used me,
abused me
and left my soul for dead?

I stand at the threshold
  and welcome hell
MY WORLD turned upside down,
              inside out
If only to feel
        the TORMENT
    to feel,
        UNDEAD within,
alive without
    a doubt

Vindicated

Surrounded by joy
and yet forlorn
Am I meant to be
a soul alone?
Why can't I feel the love
so freely given
or, see the purpose
for which I'm driven?
Perhaps this is all
I am meant to be
Perhaps it's time
to set you free
The easy way out
or the braver choice
Am I a coward
or have I found my voice?
Will I ever know
what is meant to be?
Will I ever understand
what you see in me?

Conflicted

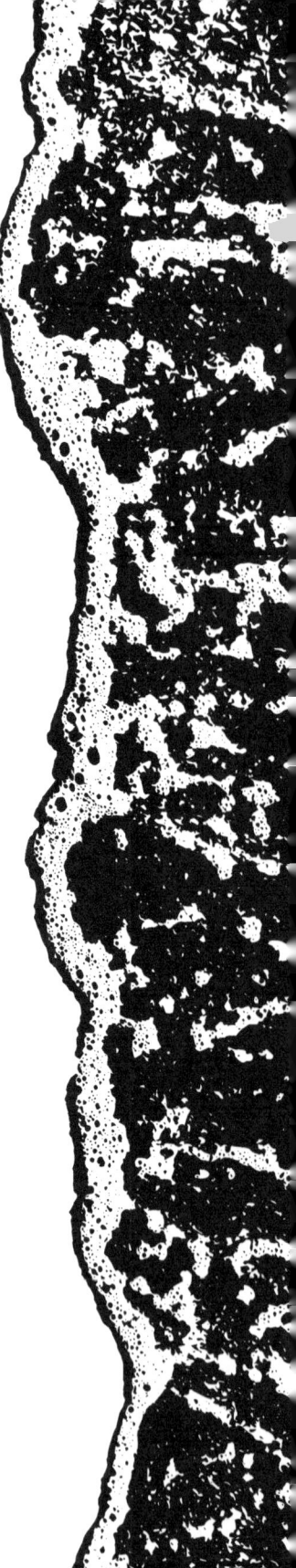

Emotions,
like the running
of the tide,
never cease
to rise or fall
If you scream
and no one hears,
were you there at all?
Swallowed
by the whirlpool,
which swirls
inside my heart
My mind
divided
another time
another place
another familiar
scary face
If you scream
and no one hears,
were you there at all?

The Tide

24

A vision, a dream
what life would be
If dreams were real,
not just a figment of a fractured mind,
a distorted distraction turned to dust,
a mirage, where life turns to sand
When the fountain of hope, runs dry
and you stretch
for the hand that never comes,
the hand just out of reach
or worse the hand retracted
The storm,
the waves crashing on the cliffs,
the precipice
the dark abyss,
the vast expansive sky
Dreams are dreams
because they could never be
before you hope
to act or die

Dreams

I gaze upon you
with love
Perspective
Perception
Bittersweet

Mourning
what could have been,
what should have been

I KNOW
the love in your eyes
What I would give
to FEEL
the love in your eyes

I gaze upon you
a reflection of me

Hatred
Remorse
Regret
Guilt
What I would give
to see just YOU
and not ME

I gaze upon you
with fear
of all the bad
that could be
and in fear
I'll steal your joy

I gaze upon you
in ANGER unexplained
When rage
boils over,
I know
my words draw blood
What I would give
to never do that again
I would stand between
you and my rage
to shield you from me

Regret

RAGE, turned inward
RAGE, well deserved

I gaze upon the sun
to feel
purity
energy,
Divine love,
joy

What I would give
to cleanse
the darkness
the shadows
the secrets
the lies
to cleanse
my tainted soul

I gaze upon the stars
to see the
infinite
heavens
beyond,
the furthest horizon

I am small, unimportant,
in the grand scheme of things

But I know
I have a purpose
I am important
I am loved

When I gaze upon you,
a reflection of me
Bittersweet

Nothing left to say
NO ANSWERS
to the questions being asked
I JUST KNOW what cannot be
and what must be
When I look to the source
OF ALL THAT IS,
with a whisper or a roar,
an avalanche begins
Where we land,
to LIVE or DIE,
is all in how
we ride
the wave

The Wave

A heart song spoken,
however brief, if heard has won
when in your heart it breathes new life
to another song yet sung

A heart song in the making
has the power to transform
matter and creation
a matter of reform

A heart song heard
to be understood
to be more than
words and melody

A heart song nurtured
like a life well lived
is a symphony of love
a testament to give

Heartsong

The power of words
The power to heal
To mend a broken heart
To lift up, to feel
The power to wound,
to tear a soul in two
To devour, to consume
To understand or misconstrue
Words are not actions
You can't see the bleeding
but to speak is to act
though you can't hear the pleading
Each word must be spoken
and chosen with care
In joy and in love,
a moment to share
With tears and in grief
in song or in prayer,
Spoken or written,
in relief or despair

The Power of Words

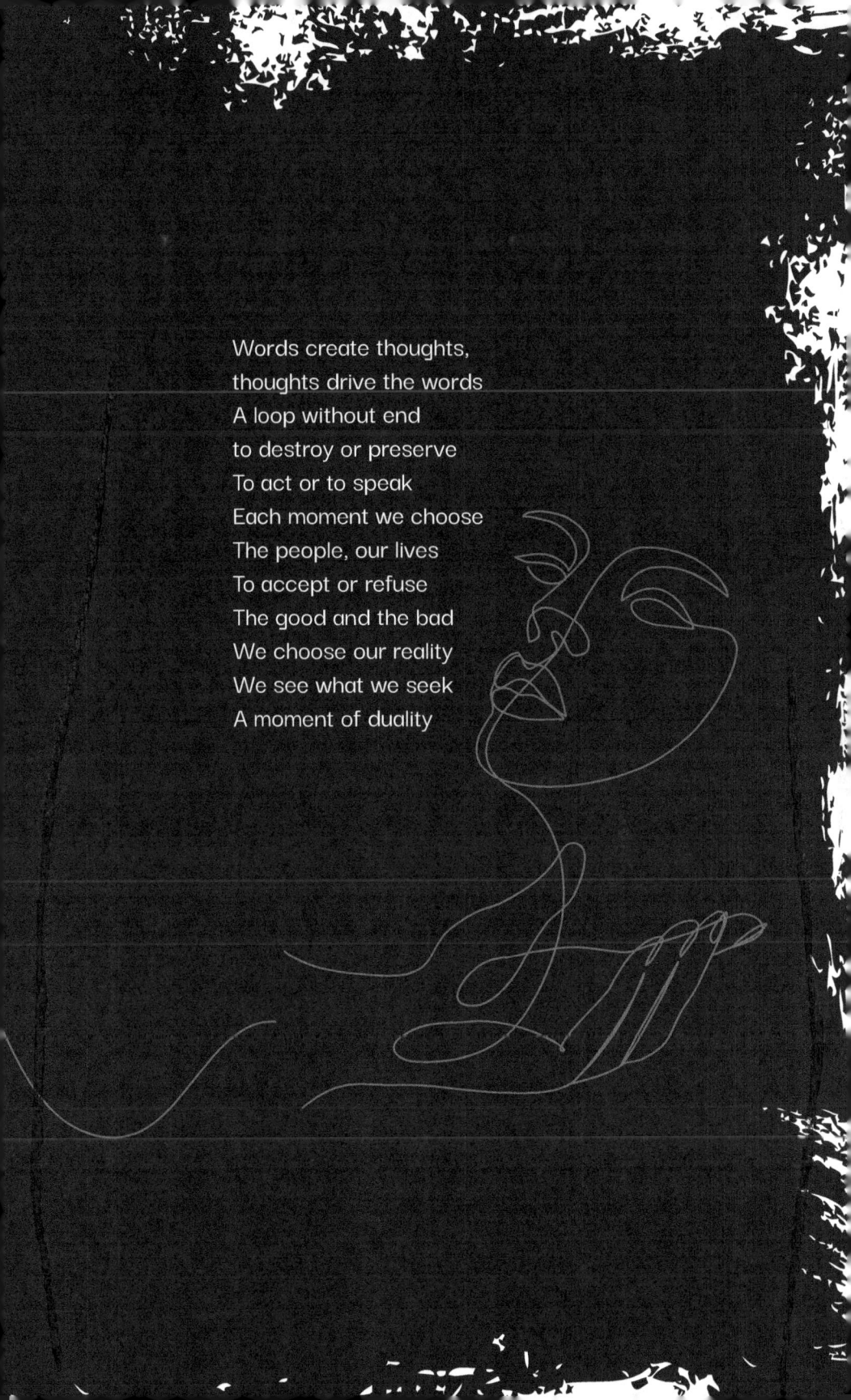

Words create thoughts,
thoughts drive the words
A loop without end
to destroy or preserve
To act or to speak
Each moment we choose
The people, our lives
To accept or refuse
The good and the bad
We choose our reality
We see what we seek
A moment of duality

So many smiles
hide so many tears
And behind all the laughs,
are mountains of fears
Like lions waiting to pounce,
to cut from the herd,
to shred every ounce
One pound of flesh,
we all do our part
Here's a piece of my soul,
a piece of my heart
What must I give
How low must I crawl
To satisfy your need
To make the innocent fall

Lions

Distorted
Contorted
for your own depravity
Sadistic
Ballistic
I was nothing but an empty shell
Perverted
Subverted
Did you know the harm you'd cause?
Shattered
Battered
How am I supposed to carry on
when my own father
couldn't see?
I was worth more
than a one-night stand
at his command
for his depravity

Depravity

A roar
demands
A whispered
command
To be held
and behold
No matter how old
I am a princess
I do what I'm told

No.

I can't breathe

No- protest
No- screams
In terror or in dreams
'No' is not allowed

Retreating to the void
to the bottomless sea
Just them and me
and nothing in between

Stifled cries
Shadows claw and draw near
In silence,
I disappear
Alone, eyes wide shut
Safe, another part of me
Numb, no one here to see
Hollow, it's not me
One more time
A hard pill to swallow

Again, and again
Choices
Still voiceless
Engulfed and divided
The trapped
and the trapper
alone and united

An Ember

Hunted and savaged
Devoured and ravaged
Consumed and defeated
Embattled, retreated
'No' is not allowed

An ember, a spark
A flame doused in the dark

Please.
Can you hear
the child pleading:
Just let me be
Just stem the bleeding
My mind divided
and defeating
Set me free
My heart
Another beating
No.
'No' is not allowed

Another voice
Another choice

Courage.
Fight.

An ember glows
The ember grows
and suddenly,
the swirl slows
My mind, my heart, my soul
A sweet repose

Be the light

"No" is not allowed

Alone
Betrayed
Unloved
Afraid
Why
did you?
How
could you?
I don't understand

I cry
no one hears
The tears
no one sees
my body
my soul
used and discarded
forgotten
in pain
left unguarded

36

It hurts

       Forget

It hurts

       Regret

It hurts

       Alone

I hurt

There's a deafening silence
in the words unspoken,
in the screams caught
in my throat
Misfired, misdirected,
a pre-programmed self-destruct

Anger
Fear
Judgment
Loathing
Stifled and festering
with nowhere to go
No one to target
except the silent child
still trapped within,
the survivor still suffering

What does it mean
to give voice
to the voiceless?
Allowing a soul
to speak its truth
compassion, understanding
empowerment
Most of all, believing
you are not alone

Cast a light
into the shadows
to see all
there is to see
Accept the child
You are not alone

Truth in the Silence

38

When I see you
and you look at me
I cease to be
INVISIBLE
Who was I
before that night
when you decided

you were MORE
THAN ME
And even in your brutality
you could never see
there was no fight
in me
YOU ONLY SAW
what you wanted
to see

Seven

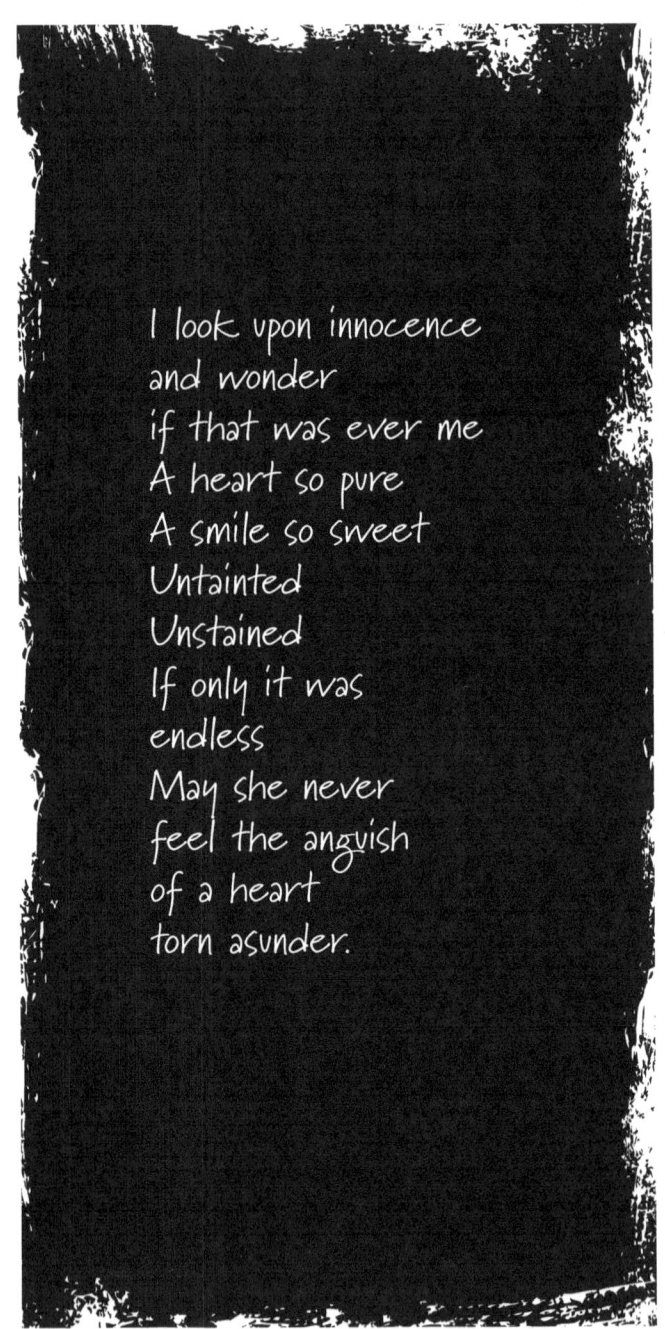

I look upon innocence
and wonder
if that was ever me
A heart so pure
A smile so sweet
Untainted
Unstained
If only it was
endless
May she never
feel the anguish
of a heart
torn asunder.

Innocence

40

How hard it is to say goodbye
to friends that touched my soul
But like the turning of the seasons,
people often come and go
And when they leave
my heart breaks
I feel alone,
I feel the ache
But every time dear friends must part,
I know that in their wake
each friend leaves soul prints
on my heart

Soul Prints

Sorrow unspoken
tears yet cried
Words twisted
turned to lies

Truth denied
when innocence died
What does it mean
to be alive?

Forget
Remember
Release
Surrender
Unleash
Breathe free

Free to be
all of me

Free

Stagnant water
where disease festers
and wounds weep
Sometimes I wish
I would sleep and never wake
How many pills
do I have to take
to make this feeling dissipate?
I stand in darkness,
refusing to see the light
This is all that I am
or will ever be-
this twisted version of me
But when you speak your truth,
I see with clarity
everything you are
and everything in me
The past is in the past
And though I feel the ache
I have to let it go
for my soul's sake
After so many years
a life of lament,
no cause to excuse,
no need to repent
Today is a new day
There is no more sorrow
Today there is hope
and a dream for tomorrow

The Past

A wish to be seen
unseen
Falling voiceless
into the void
beneath
The heart of the matter
no matter
once consumed, is doomed
to suffer,
to suffocate
under the weight
too much to bare
A wound
inflicted by the beast himself,
condemned to die
Shattered and battered
in fragments of a soul remains
Prey or predator,
a choice to blame or mourn,
To give and take
or forgive and forget
advice to transform
The pain revealed
a choice by choice
Unknown, what's real
What will it take
to make bliss
you feel
surreal, just out of reach
Surrender, it's not too late
There's doubt,
no doubt

A Wish

Confused, conflicted, connected
A fight to breathe
Contented, except
Accept
ENOUGH
to live, choose life
Ask why, what and how
to reach for what is right
and yours to take
An offense,
defense less, more or less
Waking, then making and twisting
Hearts pounding, fear,
a wave, a tsunami overtaking
in chaos
The walls and the guard towers fall
Disarmed and alarmed
to feel
For once
you feel
Twice removed
and liberated
The past, goodbye
The truth, a choice
to take
Once spoken,
a choice
to be
A voice, unseen
no more
I am me.

What if this is all of me?
What if I never cease to be
broken beyond repair?
With failure in your eyes,
would you count the lies
you think I've told
when I promised gold?
Or, would you see the truth
of who I hoped to be
when I became the all of me?
But what if this is all
I'll ever be?
What do you see
as I stand in front of you?
What would you do
if you were me?

In the Labyrinth

I wake up,
battered
In the darkness,
shattered
In the silence,
only whispers
Tormented, I am lost.

Standing
Slowly bleeding
In my mind,
my soul deceiving
Truth twisted
turned to lies
Confused, I am lost

Restrained
Restricted
Stifled
Constricted
Tied and tethered
Trapped in terror
Muted, I am lost

A monster
in silence
Whispers
Compliance
Fawn. Fight.
Freeze. Flight
Hunted, I am lost.

It's futile to feel
the warmth,
the breeze
to see the sunlight
dance through the trees
An illusion, a mirage
In fantasy, I am lost.

I am but a hologram,
a Dali distorted fantasy
of what could have been,
what should have been,
what would have been
if I had not been
Fractured, I am lost

I tire of the fight,
tire of the pain
Shattered, trapped
Escape, fall, fail
adrift
in darkness,
the nothing,
the precipice—
the only peace I see
Defeated, I am lost

Lost in the labyrinth of my mind

A silent scream
to the deaf,
numb, and blind

Gasp,
no tears

Gasp,
no sound

Gasp,
nothing

Voiceless,
a soul broken

Insignificant,
a soul divided

Soul Divided

Truth
I can't
deny
Truth
refuse
to see
Believe
this is
It is
Me

Guilt
Fault
Ceaseless
Blame
Condemned
to feel
perpetual pain

Brand me
not
Noble,
Survivor,
Victim,
Prey,
Villain
my role
to play

I stand
accused
I fall
indicted
shame
ignited
snuffed
to be
righted

Crimson
pale
dark as night

I fade
by
morning light

Villain

51

The Demon, the Phoenix, and the Ward

On sleepless nights,
When demons fight
to reign
in vain,
to give
and reciprocate:
Will they ever cease
to maim
the phoenix?
It yearns to rise
It burns
flame after flame,
in cinders and in ash
Endured pain
The demons take
The light
The ward in flight
when darkness falls

Chaos
Bloodshed
Anger
Consequences
A war
where I am
the only casualty
Bystanders
bleed
and the innocent cry
A rattling breath,
a shaky sigh
I didn't really want to die
Will you mourn me
when I'm gone?
Or will you rejoice
because it is done?

When Hope is Gone

The clouds
so dark and grey
enveloping the skies
dousing rays of light
all hope for today dies
As the raven speaks
a song of lament,
what could have been,
what cannot be...
The dream from yesterday,
vanished and vanquished
by the shadows of today
A quiet stillness
standing at the grave
When death is near,
'Why?' asks the crooning of the crow
But no one hears
the desperate cry,
the crimson tears
when terror reigns
a night of fears
A welcome respite,
when death appears
with open arms
Enveloped and slashed,
all hope is dashed—
The raven and the crow

Birds of Prey

55

Shadows in the darkness
where only the prince reigns
There's a darkness in the shadow
He's here for me
Who am I to deny him?
Who am I to crawl to the light,
when he walks through the door?
Where was I before?
Where do I go from here?
Does anyone know?
Where to go from here?
Lost in the darkness
Now just one of the shadows
Can anyone hear my cry?

No one can see
Hide your tears
No one can know
all of your fears
Sleep child of the darkness
this is where you belong
No one can save you
from me
No one can save you
from you

Silhouette

You are the monster
You are the beast
You are predator and prey
Haunted, hunted
Frozen in fear
There's nowhere to go from here
You know there's only one way out
There's only one way out

SILENCE
MASTER OF DECEIT
YOU HOLD NO POWER HERE

Is that so?

NOT AS LONG AS I AM NEAR
THIS IS MY CHILD
THIS IS MY WARD
I WILL NOT ALLOW YOU HERE

What should I do?

SLEEP CHILD OF THE DARKNESS
YOUR TIME HAS COME
NO MORE BATTLES TO BE FOUGHT OR WON
BE AT PEACE
BE WHAT YOU WERE MEANT TO BE
SHINE, CAST THE FEAR AWAY

Can you hear the silent cry
turned to rage unexplained?
And from a place of pain,
I drown,
wearing an iron crown
Despair
Sit on the throne of lies
A moan,
a mournful cry
Alone
by accident or design
Fealty
Severed and abandoned
Loyalty
Demanded and deserved
Undeserving, observed
Unlovable
Unloving
Broken
No skillful mending
Nothing
No amount of tending
What is needed
is an ending
The happily ever after
The day after
No more pain
No more sorrow
No today
No tomorrow

Happily Ever After

Alone-
yet one of many
The lost
The forgotten
The ones
destined to lose
themselves,
to numb
the pain
In agony,
relentless,
we languish
What would it take
to vanquish
the monsters?
Fragments of memories
that haunt
our anguished minds

One of Many

This life is not meant
to win or lose
Though that is a struggle
you quite often choose
To love and to live
is simply to be
You are who you are,
just as I am just me
That is all that is needed
It's time to set free
Expectations and rules
of what you should be
and to know
it's enough
Simply to be

One lonely broken soul
One tattered bleeding heart
One shattered downcast stare
Each a missing part
One battered weathered body,
often rented and abused
One fractured tiny smile,
minimally used
Are there any takers?
No offer is refused
Here's a full disclosure:
I don't want to be accused
No deception or misconception
No need to be deluded
The past, the present,
all baggage is included
Missing parts, sold as is
Not looking for a donor
Everything must go
For sale by owner

For Sale by Owner

There are times when I feel
SHATTERED,
BROKEN beyond repair
But I am reminded,
through LOVE
and ACCEPTANCE,
even the *broken*
can be WHOLE again
I have come to accept
that perhaps I was
never meant to be
A teacup
And through my broken
PIECES
may you see
the *beauty*
of the MOSAIC
when I am me.

A Mosaic

Sometimes my life's journey
feels lonely and bleak,
when I walk blindly
and don't know what I seek
With every step I take,
I get closer to the brink
But when I meet
a fellow traveler,
in this thing we call life,
we can share the burden,
we can share the strife
Together we go farther
than we could ever go alone
Together, then a part
we can find a place
to call our home

Fellow Traveler

Passion, is more than
just a belief
It's a desire
to be more
to inspire
Your life is meant to be
I hope that you can see
you alter lives
just by being you
With who you are,
not what you do
Your heart beats
a melody
For all to hear
A symphony,
it's more than
just a song
it's where your heart belongs
Giving hope
to those you meet
to all that hear the beat

So, when you think
no one will hear
remember me
and what happened here
When you spoke
and changed my life
Because you took the time to care
To share
your thoughts, so kind
your words, your rhyme
Inspired by the soul
your anthem and
the way you roll
you soar above it all
I know
the hope you bring
Will never fall,
When you are you

Passion

It is easy to forget
that there is order
to the disorder
A notion I once
believed to be naivete
But as I sit here,
in the stillness
of this day,
this minute,
this moment
in time,
I am reminded
that things are neither
good nor bad
That it is I
who chooses
to be happy or sad
I am reminded
that any peace
I choose to see,
starts with a spark within-
A piece of me

Chaos in Order

Climbing from the dark abyss,
shadows lurking, closing in
Sinister whispers, haunting and taunting
another attack
Crimson claw marks streak my back
One by one, they tear me down
A shadow, a cage, a thorny crown
A torrent of tears
A sea of sins
A whirlpool of fears
Wading and diving,
deep within
the depths
where demons
don't cease
to win
Heart, mind and soul
Once again, I fall

Climbing

Yet through it all I know
when I cast my eyes
to the stars,
the skies,
to the infinite universe,
to all that is,
once again
I am reminded:
Dark exists
so light
may shine
I breathe
I clear my mind
Bruised and scared
Pockmarked and marred
I stand
I know
I am meant to shine
To light the way,
to understand
the depths of hell
The significance of today
The story to tell
so that I may say
I am strong
I am loved
I am worthy
I am you and you are me

A moment of clarity
Magic suspended in time
Where dreams and possibilities are seen
and doubt simply falls away
A heart song knows no time or place
or wild wide-open space
or, a tiny chamber of the heart
Where does it start?
Where does it belong?
Hear a longing lonesome cry,
an ever-somber melody,
an enormous joyous symphony
Does it belong to me
or is it meant to be?
A seed planted inside the soil
of a soul yet to be seen
Where does it begin?
Where does it end?
Does it hold the power to mend
other souls wounded
meant to hear,
to see the truth of who you are,
the truth of what could be?
If only they could see
everything that was clear to me
This melancholy day
this wonderful, joyful
ordinary day
What would you say
if you could speak?
Sing

Clarity

Sacred

What is sacred?
The holy
The divine
If we are made
in the image
of that which is
sacred,
does that mean
we are sacred too?
Is it true
our body is
a temple?
If so,
is self-love
a prayer?
What does it mean
to loath ourselves?
The very fiber of
our being
is hatred—
a desecration
of who we are
—

If we are indeed sacred.

Not broken
Not warped
Transformed
Like weathered wood
or a river stone
I will not pretend
to be what I am not:
A diamond in the rough
A princess within the frog
I am flawed
But where there is pain,
there is healing
Where there are scars,
there is understanding
I may not know
where you have been,
what you have seen
but I know pain,
compassion,
and empathy
For I have been
where most have not
The journey to hell
and back again
A path I know by heart

Refined

In a fraction of an instant
where embers turn to ash
and life collides,
magic and fantasy
suspend in disbelief
See the phoenix rise

I know all that is
is meant to be
That is the peace
in the pieces of you and me
When I see you gaze upon the
starlit sky
and the look upon your face,
in the wild and open space,
your eye-
it had a spark
yet to be seen
Let your dreams soar.

A spark

Veronika Childs is an author, speaker, podcast host, and mother. She is an outspoken advocate for mental health awareness and childhood trauma recovery. Through her creative projects she hopes to encourage others to follow their passions and make a positive impact by *healing it forward.*

After experiencing a significant amount of childhood trauma, Veronika spent most of her life living on the sidelines. In 2019, Veronika had a health scare that became a catalyst for change in her life; by sharing her story, she brought abuse out of the shadows. Now, through the characters and themes in her poems and stories, she hopes to be a voice for others like herself. If only to let others know they are not alone in their pain.

www.ingramcontent.com/pod-product-compliance
Lightning Source LLC
Chambersburg PA
CBHW060351130626
46553CB00003B/1184